BUILDING AMAZING STRUC

Skyscrapers

Chris Oxlade

Heinemann
LIBRARY

H www.heinemann.co.uk
Visit our website to find out more information about Heinemann Library books.

To order:
☎ Phone 44 (0) 1865 888066
📄 Send a fax to 44 (0) 1865 314091
💻 Visit the Heinemann Bookshop at www.heinemann.co.uk to browse our catalogue and order online.

First published in Great Britain by Heinemann Library, Halley Court, Jordan Hill, Oxford OX2 8EJ
a division of Reed Educational and Professional Publishing Ltd.
Heinemann is a registered trademark of Reed Educational & Professional Publishing Ltd.

OXFORD MELBOURNE AUCKLAND JOHANNESBURG BLANTYRE
GABORONE IBADAN PORTSMOUTH (NH) USA CHICAGO

Designed by Celia Floyd
Ilustrations by Barry Atkinson
Originated by Repro Multi Warna
Printed by Wing King Tong in Hong Kong

ISBN 0 431 10972 9 (hardback)   ISBN 0 431 10979 6 (paperback)
05 04 03 02 01   05 04 03 02 01
10 9 8 7 6 5 4 3 2 1   10 9 8 7 6 5 4 3 2 1

British Library Cataloguing in Publication Data

Oxlade, Chris
    Skyscrapers. – (Building amazing structures)
    1. Skyscrapers – Design and construction – Juvenile literature
    I. Title
    720.4'83

Acknowledgements
The Publishers would like to thank the following for permission to reproduce photographs:
Associated Press, p. 26; Eye Ubiquitous, pp. 19, (Kevin Nicol) p. 16, (Michael Reed) p. 29; Frank Spooner (Basin Ajansi) p. 27; Hutchison Library (Bernard Regent) p.15, (Jeremy Horner) p 6; J Allan Cash Ltd, pp. 4, 8, 25; James Davies Travel Photography, pp. 5, 20; Robert Harding, pp. 11, 24; Taylor Woodrow, p 23; Tony Stone pp. 22, (Cosmo Condina) p. 7, (Glen Allison) p. 10, (Joel Rogers) p 21.

Cover photograph reproduced with permission of Robert Harding Picture Library.

Every effort has been made to contact copyright holders of any material reproduced in this book. Any omissions will be rectified in subsequent printings if notice is given to the Publisher.

Words appearing in the text in bold, **like this**, are explained in the Glossary.

Contents

About skyscrapers

A skyscraper is a very tall building with dozens of floors where thousands of people live or work. The name 'skyscraper' is normally given to buildings that have more than forty storeys (floors).

A skyscraper is a type of structure. A structure is an object that is built to resist a push or a pull. A skyscraper is a structure because it resists the weight of the people, furniture or office equipment pushing downwards on its floors.

There are dozens of skyscrapers around the world that tower more than 300 m into the sky. From the tops of these incredible structures you can see far into the distance, and people in the streets below look like tiny ants.

So why do we build skyscrapers? Who decides to build them and who designs them? How are they built, what materials are needed, and what special machines?

The twin towers of the Petronas Towers in Kuala Lumpur, Malaysia, the world's tallest skyscraper, are linked by a dramatic 'skybridge'.

Why do we build skyscrapers?

Finding space to build offices and flats in busy city centres is difficult. A skyscraper only takes up a small amount of space on the ground, but it creates a huge amount of floor space inside. A fifty-storey skyscraper contains as much flat space as fifteen soccer pitches.

Most skyscrapers are used for offices, some are residential (used for living in), and some are used for hotels and shopping. Some contain floors with a mixture of offices, flats and shops. The tallest skyscrapers are often built by companies or city authorities because of the pride skyscrapers attract.

The 417-m-high World Trade Center in New York, USA, contains more floor space than any other skyscraper.

FACTS ✤ It's a skyscraper world record!
- Tallest skyscraper: Petronas Towers, Kuala Lumpur, Malaysia.
  Height: 452 m (which includes its tall pinnacles). If the tower was on its side, it would take five minutes to walk along it!
- Largest number of floors: Sears Tower, Chicago, USA.
  Number of floors: 110. Height: 443 m.
- Most space inside: World Trade Center, New York, USA.
  Area: 880,000 square m (that's about the same as 220 soccer pitches). Height: 417 m.

Buildings with several floors were first needed in the 1850s in the big cities of the USA, such as New York and Chicago. Land was becoming very expensive, and high-rise building could create plenty of office space on a small plot of land. Buildings with stone or brick walls could be up to five storeys high. After that the lower walls had to be so thick to support the floors above that there was not much space left for rooms!

Two things were needed for taller buildings. One was an iron **frame** of **columns** and **beams** to support the

floors. The second was a safe passenger lift, which could carry people to the top floors. Another important step came in the 1860s, when a process was developed to make **steel**. Steel is stronger and lighter than iron, and it could be used to make strong, thin skyscraper frames. **Concrete** frames for skyscrapers were first used in the early 20th century.

The Flat Iron Building, New York, completed in 1903, was one of the earliest steel-framed skyscrapers.

The first skyscraper

In 1885 American **architect** William Le Baron Jenney built a ten-storey office building in Chicago called the Home Insurance Company Building. It was the first building to have a steel frame, and was the first real skyscraper. The word 'skyscraper' was first used in the 1880s. Skyscrapers quickly became higher and higher. The 381 m, 85-storey Empire State Building, completed in 1931, is still one of the highest skyscrapers in the world.

The mast of New York's Empire State Building was originally designed as a mooring for giant passenger airships.

Moving up and down

Any building with more than about ten storeys would be unpractical without mechanical lifts. Walking to the top of a skyscraper such as the Empire State Building, with its 1800 steps, would take half an hour! The first safety lift (which would not fall to the bottom of its shaft if the cable broke) was invented by American Elisha Otis in the 1850s. This was powered by steam. Electric lifts were developed in the 1880s.

Foundations

All skyscrapers have the same basic structure. The floors and walls are supported by a strong **steel** or **concrete frame**. The frame rests on **foundations** that carry the massive weight of the skyscraper into the ground. They stop it sinking into the ground or toppling over.

Down to the bedrock

Deep underground there is always hard, solid rock, called **bedrock**. Sometimes the bedrock reaches right to the surface, but normally it is covered with layers of softer rocks, such as clay, and a layer of very soft topsoil.

Piles and slabs

If the bedrock is near the surface, the soft soil is removed and concrete foundations for the frame are built on top of it. If the bedrock is deeper down, steel or concrete **columns** called **piles** reach down through the softer layers to the bedrock beneath. The columns of the frame rest on top of the piles. Sometimes a huge box called a **caisson** is sunk down to the bedrock and filled with concrete to form a foundation.

This machine is being used to dig a deep hole for a pile foundation.

Sometimes the bedrock is too deep underground for piles to reach. In this case the skyscraper frame must rest on softer rocks. If the skyscraper rested straight on top of this rock, the columns could gradually sink into the ground. Eventually it could topple sideways. So the weight of the skyscraper must be spread out over a large area of ground to reduce the pressure on the ground. It must rest on a large **reinforced concrete, slab foundation**, much wider than the building.

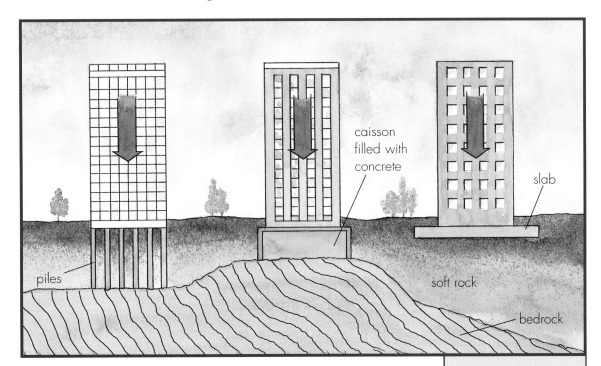

caisson filled with concrete

slab

piles

soft rock

bedrock

TRY THIS

Stand on a slab

For this experiment, you need to find some soft soil or sand that you can stand on, such as a thick layer of soil in an old tray. Stand on one leg in the soil. How far does your foot sink in? Now lay a piece of wood bigger than your shoe on the soil and try again. This time your foot will not sink in so far. The wood acts like a slab foundation, spreading your weight.

These are the three main types of skyscraper foundation. The red arrows show the strong downwards force.

Skyscraper frames

All skyscrapers have a **steel** or **concrete frame**. The frame supports the external **curtain walls**, the internal walls, the floors, and everything on the floors, such as the furniture and people.

Members of the frame

The frame is made up of **vertical** pieces called **columns** and **horizontal** pieces called **beams**. Each column and beam is called a **member**. The columns support the ends of the beams, and the beams support the floors. So the weight from the floors goes along the beams and down the columns. The beams must resist bending and the columns must resist being squashed.

Architects often make the frame part of a skyscraper's design. You can clearly see the bracing in the frame of the Bank of China, Hong Kong.

The columns on each floor support the weight from all the floors above, so the columns at the bottom of the frame must be much stronger than the columns further up. The frame itself is very heavy. The steel frame of the Empire State Building weighs 57,000 tonnes, which is about one-sixth of the weight of the whole building.

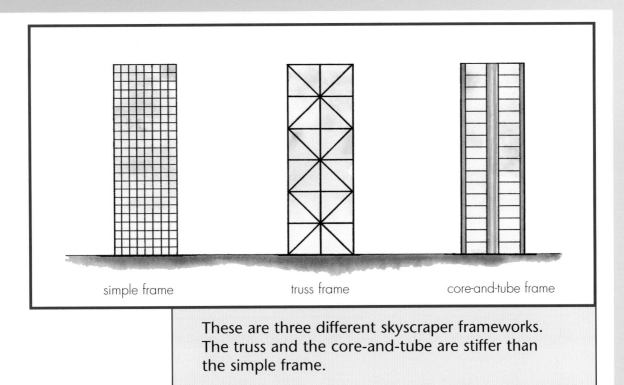

simple frame   truss frame   core-and-tube frame

These are three different skyscraper frameworks. The truss and the core-and-tube are stiffer than the simple frame.

Flooring and cladding

Skyscraper floors are slabs of **reinforced concrete** supported on their edges by the beams of the frame. The external walls are called curtain walls because they hang from the frame. The material used for them is called **cladding**.

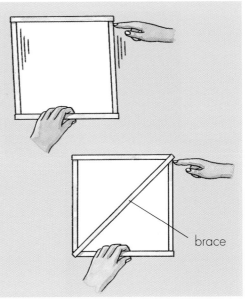

TRY THIS

Bracing a frame
Bracing makes a frame stiffer. Cut four pieces of thick card 20 × 1 cm. Glue the pieces end-to-end to make a square frame. Stand the frame on one edge and push sideways on one top corner. If you push hard enough, the square will collapse sideways. Re-glue the frame and glue another length of card diagonally across the frame. Try pushing sideways again. The braced frame is much stronger.

brace

Skyscraper Services

Like any other office or block of flats, a skyscraper needs **services** such as water supplies and electricity supplies – but more of them! As many people can live and work in a big skyscraper as can in a small town. Some services are special to skyscrapers, such as high-speed lifts and air conditioning.

Services are needed on every floor of a skyscraper. Pipes, cables and lift **shafts** are contained in a service **core** which stretches through every floor from the basement to the roof. Cables and pipes spread out across the floors from the core.

Air conditioning machinery is usually placed on the skyscraper roof, where it has a supply of fresh air.

Whizzing up and down

Skyscrapers need dozens of lifts to move people up to their floors and back to the ground. Express lifts carry people direct to 'sky' lobbies on the upper floors. Slow lifts stop at every floor in a group, linking the sky lobbies together. The World Trade Center has a staggering 99 lifts in each tower! The lifts in the John Hancock Center travel at 549 m per minute – that's nearly three floors a second!

A computer decides which lift to send when somebody presses a button. There are always stairs too, which are used if the lifts break down.

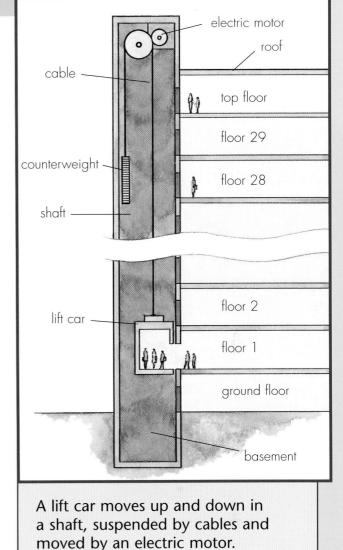

A lift car moves up and down in a shaft, suspended by cables and moved by an electric motor.

Servicing a town in the air

The main services needed in a skyscraper are water supply, electricity supply, air conditioning and communications, such as telephone lines. Water comes from storage tanks at the top of the building. Powerful pumps are needed to move the water up to the tanks in the first place. An air conditioning system keeps the air in the whole building clean and at a comfortable temperature and **humidity**. The air is carried around the building in large pipes called ducts. A skyscraper normally has its own electricity **generators** in case of power cuts.

Skyscraper materials

The main materials used in skyscraper structures are **steel** and **concrete**. Steel is an **alloy** made mostly of iron. Steel is used to make the **members** of a steel **frame** because it is extremely strong. For example, a steel cable as thick as your finger could lift a 30-tonne truck without snapping.

Uncrushable concrete

Concrete consists of **cement**, water and aggregate, which is made up of sand and gravel. When the ingredients are first mixed, the concrete is liquid. The cement and water react together and then become a solid which binds the aggregate together. Concrete is so strong that you could put a fully-loaded jumbo jet on a house-brick-sized piece of concrete without crushing the concrete.

Concrete is only strong when you try to squash it (when it is in compression). So steel bars are added to any part of a structure made from concrete that will be stretched. This new material is called **reinforced concrete**.

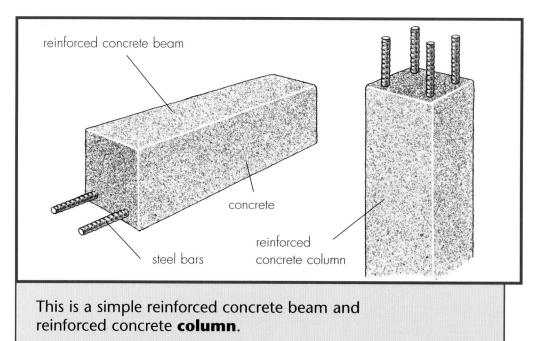

reinforced concrete beam

concrete

steel bars

reinforced concrete column

This is a simple reinforced concrete beam and reinforced concrete **column**.

On the outside

The **cladding** materials must be light, strong, weatherproof and attractive. They include brick, stone (which is cut into thin sheets), glass, and metals such as aluminium and stainless steel. The metals used must not corrode (lose their appearance and strength because of the actions of rainwater and air). Special coatings are put on the glass to stop too much heat from the sun entering the building.

This New York skyscraper has red polished stone cladding at the base and glass cladding above.

TRY THIS

Block and paper beams

A row of toy building blocks (or small blocks of wood) placed end to end is like a concrete **beam**. It is very strong if you try to squash its ends together, but breaks up if you try to pull its ends apart. A piece of paper is like a steel rod. It is quite strong if you try to pull its ends apart, but buckles if you try to squash its ends together. But if you tape the paper under the row of blocks (as shown), you make a strong beam!

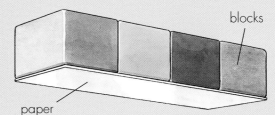

blocks

paper

Designing a skyscraper

When an organization has decided that it needs to build a skyscraper, it asks a company of **architects** to design the building for them. It gives the architects an idea of the sort of building they want and how much they want to spend.

The architects also need to know how much space is required inside the skyscraper.

The architect of the waterfront skyscraper in Dubai has designed the windows to look like a huge sail.

Sorting out the structure

Once the architects have decided the shape and style of the skyscraper, a **structural engineer** designs it. The skyscraper structure needs to support the weight of the people and furniture on the floors (called the live **loads**), and the weight of the parts of the skyscraper itself (called the dead loads).

The structure must also resist strong winds blowing against its sides. The push of the wind is called wind load. Wind loads are greater than you might think – the tops of the tallest skyscrapers sway slowly by more than half a metre from side to side in strong winds.

The design of a skyscraper is fed into a computer, which can show what the finished building will look like.

Fixtures and fittings

Once the structure is designed, all the other parts must be designed too, from the fixtures for the **cladding** to the bathrooms on each floor and the decorations in the lobby. Light fittings, lifts and water pipes must also be chosen. A large team of designers and engineers is needed to do the work. Once the design is complete, drawings and documents are prepared.

The sky is the limit

The Sears Tower, 443 m high and completed in 1973, is still the second tallest building in the world. Modern design and construction methods would allow a building at least 1000 m high to be built. So why hasn't one been built this high? The answer is that it would be too expensive. Another reason is that extremely tall buildings would sway badly in strong winds, making the people in them feel sick.

Preparing the site

The enormous project of building a skyscraper can take several years to complete. One engineering company, called the main contractor, oversees the whole construction job. It may do some of the work itself, but many smaller companies called **sub-contractors**, are employed to do special jobs, such as making sections of the **frame** or installing lifts.

New skyscrapers are normally built in busy city centres. For safety, the building site is closed off with strong fencing. Old buildings on the site have to be demolished.

Laying the foundations

The first stage in laying the **foundations** is to remove any soft topsoil from the site. This is done by excavating machines and dump trucks which carry the soil away. Digging a deep hole can make the foundations of nearby buildings move, so a thick wall called a **diaphragm wall** is often built in the ground around the site first.

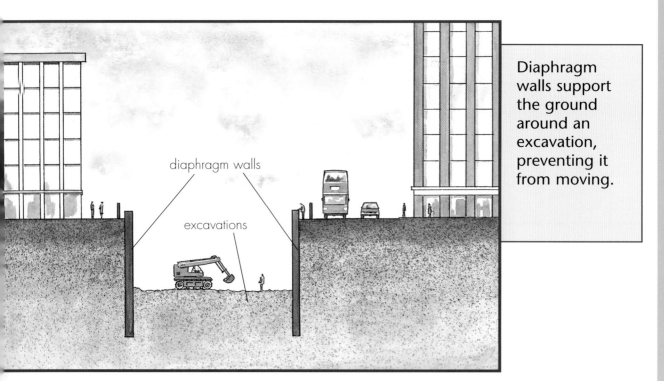

diaphragm walls

excavations

Diaphragm walls support the ground around an excavation, preventing it from moving.

Here you can see the bottom **columns** of a new building being placed on top of completed pile foundations.

Next, the foundations are put in the ground. If a **slab foundation** is being used, reinforcing **steel** is put in place and **concrete** is poured round it until the concrete reaches the correct depth. Steel is left sticking out of the concrete for the frame to be attached to. If **pile** foundations are being used, they have to be sunk into the ground. Ready-made piles are driven into the ground with a pile-driving machine. *In situ* piles are built by digging holes with a machine called an auger. The holes are then filled with **reinforced concrete**.

If pile foundations are used, the soil between the piles is excavated and floors are added to make a basement, which is often used for a car park and to house machinery for the **services**, such as air conditioning equipment.

19

Erecting the frame

With firm **foundations** in place, work can start on the skyscraper's supporting **frame**. The very bottom sections of the frame are connected to the foundations, so that the frame cannot move about or topple over.

Giant jigsaws

The **members** of a **steel** frame are made up of flat pieces of steel **welded** together and cut to the correct length. They are prefabricated (made in advance) in a factory, delivered to the site and put together like a giant jigsaw puzzle.

Each member is numbered so that everybody knows where it goes. It has holes drilled in it ready to be bolted to the other parts with special high-strength nuts and bolts. Some frames are welded together instead. The workers who put the frame together wear safety harnesses and need a good head for heights!

The frame of the Chicago Beach Hotel, Dubai, has a combined steel and concrete frame.

Massive moulds

Concrete frames are normally built *in situ* by pouring concrete into wooden or metal moulds called **formwork**. Bars of steel reinforcement are put inside the formwork and the concrete is poured around them. Bars are left poking out of the **beams** and **columns** for the next sections to be attached to. A concrete **core** is often built by a method called **slip-casting**. The formwork for the core gradually creeps upwards as concrete is poured in the top and set when it reaches the bottom.

Here you can see the metal formwork and completed columns formed by pouring concrete into the moulds.

Mechanical helpers

All the materials for a frame, such as steel beams and columns, and concrete for the floors, have to be lifted to where they are needed. Tall construction cranes do most of the lifting.

Fresh, runny concrete is lifted by cranes in huge skips, or pumped up in thick pipes. Temporary lifts called hoists are connected to the outside of the frame to carry workers and materials up the skyscraper.

Floors, walls and services

As the **frame** for each floor of the skyscraper is completed, work starts on the floor itself, then the **cladding** is added. This makes the floor below weatherproof, so work can start on installing **services**, such as water pipes and electricity cables. The lower floors of the building are often ready to use before the frame of the top floor is complete.

Pouring floors and adding cladding

Floors work like very wide **beams**, passing the **load** on them to the beams of the frame. They are made by pouring concrete on to steel **decks**. Making the floors in this way is quick because no **formwork** is needed. Flights of stairs between the floors are also added at this stage. They, too, are made of **reinforced concrete**.

Cladding is attached to the outside of the frame in sections, which might be huge panes of glass or thin sheets of metal. Strong fastenings are needed to stop the cladding blowing off in high winds. Narrow strips of rubber are placed between the sections of cladding to stop water leaking through.

A skyscraper floor is made by pouring concrete onto a deck formed by corrugated steel plates.

Installing services

Hundreds of people working for dozens of **sub-contractors** move into the empty floors to start installing the hundreds of pieces of equipment needed to make the skyscraper useable. These include lifts, toilets, electricity **generators**, water tanks, waste-disposal chutes and air conditioning plants. Hundreds of kilometres of pipes, cables and ducts are needed to connect everything together. These are fitted under each floor and hidden when the ceiling panels are added.

Thin internal walls are added to divide the floors into rooms, the decorating is done and the carpets are laid. At last the skyscraper is ready for its occupants.

Stopping a meltdown

Steel loses its strength if it gets very hot. At 400°C (twice the temperature in a hot oven) it is only half as strong as at room temperature. To prevent steel skyscraper frames from weakening in a fire, the steel **members** are sprayed with a coating of fire-resistant material.

A section of cladding is lifted into place on a skyscraper.

Skyscrapers in use

Work on a skyscraper does not finish when the building work is complete. Dozens of people are needed to maintain the skyscraper and keep it running smoothly, from receptionists and cleaners to electricians and plumbers.

Day in, day out

The day-to-day maintenance of a skyscraper includes cleaning offices and flats, lobbies and lifts, removing rubbish and delivering post and supplies to each floor. The jobs are the same as for other buildings, but on a much bigger scale. So skyscrapers often have their own waste-disposal plants and post offices. Maintenance workers are always on hand to make repairs.

Window cleaning is the trickiest job, especially on the outside! It's a long job – the World Trade Center has 43,600 windows! By the time the cleaners have finished, it is time to start again.

Window cleaning cradles hang on cables attached to a track that runs around the edge of the roof.

In an emergency

The worst events in a skyscraper are power cuts and fires. In a power cut, lifts can stop between floors, trapping people inside. So emergency **generators** start working and provide power for each lift to be moved to the ground and for emergency lighting.

Smoke detectors automatically detect a fire starting anywhere in the skyscraper. Sprinklers automatically spray water onto the fire. In a fire, the lifts are set to stop at the next floor they come to so that people do not get trapped if the power fails. Everybody evacuates the building using the stairs, and fire teams fight the fire with the hose reels that are situated on each floor.

This is the foyer of the World Trade Center, in New York. More than 50,000 people move in and out of the building every day.

Skyscrapers that went wrong

Skyscrapers are designed to carry heavy **loads** of people and equipment without falling over or sinking into the ground, to withstand hurricane-force winds and strong earthquakes, and to keep their inhabitants safe in case of fire. So far there have been no major disasters in skyscrapers, but there have been some accidents.

Skyscrapers that survived

Two skyscrapers in New York have survived events that you would think might have knocked them down. In 1945, during foggy weather, a huge B-25 bomber flew straight into the Empire State Building at the level of the 78th floor. Several people in the building were killed, as well as the aircraft's crew. But the building's **steel frame** withstood the collision.

In 1993, a massive terrorist bomb exploded in the underground car park in the basement of the north tower of the World Trade Center in New York. The 417 m tower was rocked by the blast and several people were killed, but the frame survived – as this photo shows.

This photograph shows how the concrete frame of a block of flats collapsed in the Turkish earthquake of 1999.

Disastrous collapses

You might think that a skyscraper would be one of the worst places to be in an earthquake but, in fact, it could be one of the safest. The strong frame inside a skyscraper can bend slightly without breaking, so it can stand up to the shaking. A building made with **piles** of heavy **masonry** would quickly be shaken apart.

However, many high-rise buildings have collapsed in earthquakes. Most have had **concrete** frames which have not been designed carefully enough. They have broken where the **beams** meet the **columns** because not enough reinforcement was used. In the huge earthquake that hit Turkey in 1999, tens of thousands of people died because their high-rise blocks of flats collapsed. In many cases this was because the builders had skimped on reinforcements to save money.

Skyscraper facts

The world's tallest skyscrapers

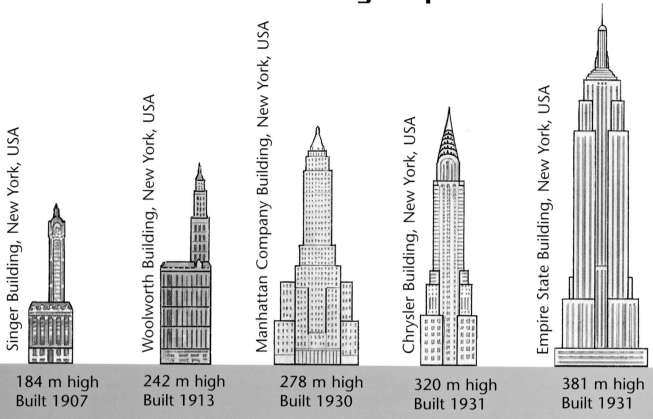

Singer Building, New York, USA
184 m high
Built 1907

Woolworth Building, New York, USA
242 m high
Built 1913

Manhattan Company Building, New York, USA
278 m high
Built 1930

Chrysler Building, New York, USA
320 m high
Built 1931

Empire State Building, New York, USA
381 m high
Built 1931

Higher and higher

The record-holder for the world's tallest skyscraper has
changed through the years. The desire to own the tallest
skyscraper has often made people build a skyscraper a
metre or two higher than another, often just by adding a thin
spire on the roof!

This diagram shows skyscrapers that have been the world's
tallest at some point. The Jin Mao Building is included
because, in 2000 it is the world's third tallest skyscraper. The
Petronas Towers is officially the world's tallest as its spires
are part of its structure, (those of the Sears Tower were
added after building). The CN Tower is shown for
comparison.

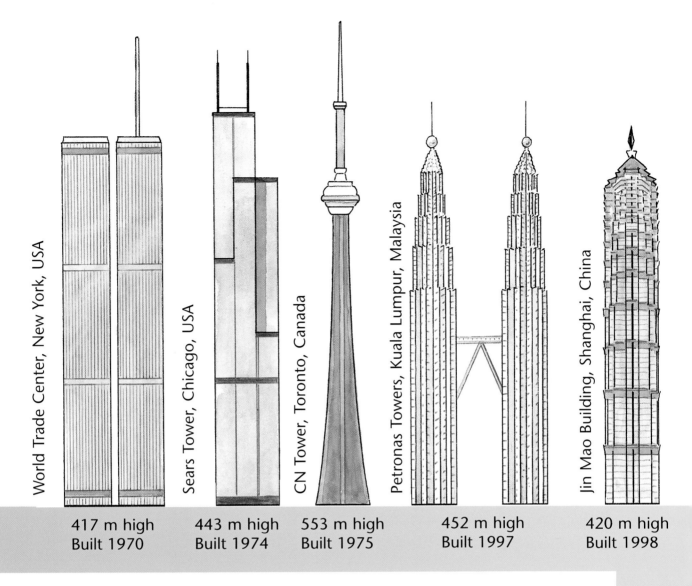

World Trade Center, New York, USA

417 m high
Built 1970

Sears Tower, Chicago, USA

443 m high
Built 1974

CN Tower, Toronto, Canada

553 m high
Built 1975

Petronas Towers, Kuala Lumpur, Malaysia

452 m high
Built 1997

Jin Mao Building, Shanghai, China

420 m high
Built 1998

World's tallest towers

Amazingly, skyscrapers are not the tallest structures in the world. Some radio and television towers are even taller. They do not have floors, but many have observation decks (or even restaurants) near the top.

The world's tallest building is the CN Tower, Toronto, Canada. The Skypod, two-thirds of the way up, contains viewing rooms, a nightclub and a restaurant.

FACTS ✜ Tall towers
- CN Tower, Toronto, Canada (1975). Height: 553 m.
- Ostankino Tower, Moscow, Russia. Height: 537 m.
- Oriental Pearl Tower, Shanghai, China. Height: 468 m.
- Menara Tower, Kuala Lumpur, Malaysia. Height: 420 m.

Glossary

alloy material made of a metal and another metal or another substance. For example, steel is an alloy made of iron with a small amount of the substance carbon.

architect person who designs the shape, appearance and internal layout of a building

beam length of steel or concrete supported at its two ends

bedrock hard, solid rock which continues deep into the Earth's crust

bracing diagonal pieces of a frame that stop the frame twisting sideways

caisson large steel or concrete box that is sunk into water and filled with concrete to form a foundation

cement mixture of chemicals that hardens into a rock-like substance after it is mixed with water. Cement is an ingredient of concrete.

cladding material used to make the external, curtain wall of a skyscraper

column vertical piece of a frame, which carries load downwards

concrete very hard material made up of cement, water and aggregate, which is made up of sand and gravel

core section in the middle of a skyscraper that goes from the ground to the roof. Services such as lifts go through the core.

curtain wall external, weatherproof wall of a skyscraper

deck area where people walk

diaphragm wall a wall in the ground around a building site that stops the earth collapsing as foundations are dug

formwork metal or wooden moulds that concrete is poured into to make beams, columns and floors

foundation structure that spreads the weight of a skyscraper and the people and equipment in it into the ground

frame structure made up of beams and columns joined together that supports the floors and walls of a skyscraper

generator device similar to an electric motor, but which does the opposite job. It turns movement into an electric current.

habitable   suitable place to live

horizontal   describes an object that is lying on its side

humidity   amount of water vapour (the gas form of water) in the air. Very dry air has low humidity. Very damp, sticky air has high humidity.

in situ   made where it will be used. In situ concrete is poured in moulds and sets where it is needed.

load   any force that acts on a skyscraper, such as the weight of the people in it or the force of wind on its side

masonry   brick, stone or concrete

member   piece of a frame, such as a beam or a column

pile   long steel or concrete pole driven deep into the ground

reinforced concrete   concrete that has steel reinforcing bars embedded in it

services   electricity supplies, water supplies, lifts, communications and so on, that make a skyscraper habitable

shaft   large lobby inside a skyscraper that stretches over several floors

slab foundation   building foundation made up of a large slab that 'floats' on top of the ground

slip-casting   a way of making a concrete column in a mould. The mould slowly creeps upwards and concrete is poured into the top. When the concrete comes out of the bottom, it is set.

steel   alloy made mostly of iron (an alloy is material made of a metal with other substances added)

structural engineer   engineer who designs the structure of a building

sub-contractor   company employed by a main contractor to carry out specialist work such as designing the parts of a skyscraper

vertical   describes an object that is standing upright

welded   when two pieces of metal have been attached to each other by heating them so much that they melt and join together when they cool

Index